Lucid Lines 2;

Rusted Heart

Lucidity Lamb

To my love,

In your eyes, I can see the sunflower future.
I never want to look away.

With love,
Luci Lamb

Contents

A Poem for My Love

Let my lips be your last touch tonight.
Think of me as you close your day.
A drowsy "I love you" will set the world right,
As we dream all our troubles far away.

I adore your energy, intellect, and grace,
And the way you love to inspire laughter.
Your heartfelt smile alights your beautiful face,
Reminding me I have found my happy ever after.

With sword and key, we made our promises to stay.
I love you in this moment as I loved you then.
And no matter the hurdles along the way,
I will treasure you, my love, until the end.

Heart Strings

Drums are quieted tonight.
The cello lays a path for sighs.
Oboes in the morning come,
But tonight, the strings are all alive.

Violas speak, joy resonates,
The double bass sings deep.
Hearts expand, clasped hands shake,
Stars explode and violins weep.

The harp brings a story of peace,
Intonations drifting up above.
If words were joined to this heartbeat,
They'd whisper, simply, "You, my love."

Rocky Horror Love

She brought my life to life.
She was beauty and intellect,
Energy and interest,
And confident femininity.

She wore a lab coat and glasses,
A pencil in her bun.
She wore striped tights and glitter,
And short skirts and bangles.

How I'd like to see her now,
My Rocky Horror Love,
But our love was only mine,
Invisible wall of heterosexuality

Holding one kind of love on my side,
And another on hers,
Like two universes sharing
A simultaneous, sensational sunrise.

Butterfly Wings

I was lost
In a collage of lilies,
Roses, and weeds;
A field drifting toward freedom as
Forgotten flowers
Were left to fulfill wild aspirations.

I saw a scarlet butterfly
Perch on the tip of
A blooming lily.
Petals and wings open,
Showing twin patterns of
Color and shape and negative space.

I saw you
Across the glamour and pollen,
Standing
On a path of clover and stone,
Your welcoming smile
A mirror of mine.

You waved as I did,
Two friends or lovers,
Strangers, in truth,
We began our

Delicate journey,
Angling and curving closer.

You spoke your mind,
And I spoke mine,
Lips and breath
Shaping our pasts and dreams.
Our words were simultaneous;
Our eyes were shy.

You saw the shape,
Of the way that we stood
On the gravel and grass beneath our feet.
Shadows joined
As distance shrank
For our embrace.

We parted and
I turned, my eyes seeking wings
As they rose in a cloud of beauty,
Delicate and strong.
In their place, a beginning,
A seed of words.

We each felt the
Magnetic pull and,
Turning,

Absorbed each other's gaze,

Each echoing a wave goodbye,

For now.

United, Adrift

Deep within a drifting dream,
And again, in dawning day,
You, my love, will be content,
Safe within my arms.

Sleep comes softly to us
Despite the oppressive din.
Without intent, the world chaotic
Melds to dreamy skies.

When we shut out the light,
Our secret souls collide.
And I and you will gently float
In a cloud's cushioning embrace.

Stay with me for the remainder
Of our lives together in peace,
Spinning round the oaken center,
United, adrift, you and me.

And She, And She

And she sparkled.

And she smiled.

And their hearts were beating, wild.

Hand in hand they

Said the words,

Joining hearts and lives and worlds.

Kiss impassioned,

Love unshaken.

Vows of her, for her, now taken.

Down the aisle,

Souls revived.

Love, eternal, sparkling, alive.

A Place I Can Call Home

Seems all my life I've been wandering,
Days and nights the same.
Maybe I'm just looking for someone
Willing to share the pain.

They say home is where the heart is,
But I can't find a place;
Someone who knows how to forgive.
Aren't I deserving of some grace?

For me it's hard to find a mate,
But I trust someday I will.
Until then, I will be alright,
Though I admit I'm lonely still.

I've looked in light and darkest places,
And in the in-between.
If I found an honest soul,
Could I even still believe?

Maybe home is where the heart is,
But I can't find my way.
I don't have a hat to hang and
Nowhere to hang it anyway.

So this is my wish for someone

Who will give me all their best;

Someone to show me that they care,

And take me home at last to rest.

Waiting

In the darkness: twining, turning.
In the fire: blinding, burning.
In the ether: falling, flying.
In the shallows: tripping, trying.

Here I live with arms spread wide,
Waiting for love to arrive,
Impassioned life, blushing grin,
Sanguine dreamscape, rushing in.

Unfair, Insufficient

I once loved a woman
Who slept with a man
I would soon marry.

I once married a man
Who slept with a woman
I would have loved for life.

I once left them both,
Friend and husband,
Unfair burdens to carry.

If only she'd loved me,
If only he'd been true,
But I could not suffice.

After Words

Persephone was struck with awe as she
Searched his wild eyes, blinking into hers.
Aidon, who'd always infuriated
And despised, held her now with compassion.

The fight was the same as it had been for years,
But the end was shockingly strange and new.
As he lay on her, catching his own breath,
Vivid truth sparked in his widened eyes.

Her surprise was less about him than her
Exhilaration at the epiphany.
Her soul thrilled as her heart beat against his.
She pressed hungry lips to his mouth once more.

His eyes closed as silence danced, enlivened
By lust and love after so many words.
Neither could comprehend what happened but,
For the first time, they both understood.

Sleeping Together

Charles found a boy and how he loved him so.
Raymond loved the way Charlie's heart would show.
In the night they spooned, hidden beneath the sheets,
Falling asleep to the rhythm of each other's heartbeat.

Garret loved to listen to his beloved's gentle snore.
Jessie clung to him, even sleeping, wanting more.
Face to face, they lay until in dreams they danced,
Entangling their limbs and lives more at every chance.

Chris and Kris found set pillows side by side.
A head on each, untouching, they closed tired eyes.
When the sun rose, they woke together in a breath,
And delighted in the one they'd love unto death.

Yellow Heart

She rose and fell in shadow.

Yellow of her crumpled dress,

The last glowing embers

Of a forgotten fire

On a night of spontaneous bliss.

They said she was not brave enough.

But she was bold as the sun,

Pretty as a fall flower,

Dewey chrysanthemum,

Blooming brightly, late, but just in time.

Yellow as the vine that rises

Behind a wall of isolation

And reaches out,

Letting condescending

Early-enders wither in shadow.

Her lemon-flavored lips kiss the dew

Of the sunray she chose

Before she rises and dances away,

In love with adventure,

But not with a solitary rose.

Jack and Jill Syndrome

There's something I call Jack and Jill Syndrome;
Follow them up that hill and right back down.
Lost as a shadow in the noon day sun.
You think you're wise, but you'll break your crown.

Tumbling down,
Head over heal,
Falling for a rotten deal.

Jack asks Jill if she will always love him.
Jill tells Jack their love will not be denied.
Jack asks Jill to follow him to glory.
And Jill promises she'll stay by his side.

Through California and through Rhode Island,
Back and forth, across the Caribbean Sea,
To Hell and back but she'll start to wonder,
Was this fairytale ever meant to be?

Spin and whirl,
Falling faster,
Where's your happy ever after?

Jill asks Jack where they're going next.
He says it doesn't matter, never will.
But when he decides to stop the climb,

Stormy winds blow them down that hill.

What does a passenger feel on that ride?
What do you do if they stop the ascent?
Do you keep climbing, or stand there screaming?
Do you fall with them, your promises kept?

Fall down,
Or stay still,
Or make your own way up that hill.

There's something I call Jack and Jill Syndrome;
Follow them up that hill and right back down.
Wishing you had been wiser sooner,
Certain it will be different next time around.

String on Fire

I love him like candlelight,
Gorgeous and delicate
In his honest soul.
My soul enlivened only
By his heat and energy.

He is my reason.
Life is his glimmering,
His vibration of ions,
His colors and shadows,
His pulsing beat.

He is the fire,
The candlewax
That surrounds me.
He makes me drip
Soul-drops of saline.

Our world is as one,
Useful to the universe
Only as long as he
Never realizes I am
Only a scrap of string.

I burn out as he fades

Away to nothing.
He is lost to shadow
And I was never real
Without him.

Tarnished Diamonds

The rose weeps pain
Into her spleen.
Rage brings cold tears
That drown her liver.

Convulsions raze
Fragile lining.
A misplaced ring
Strangles her heart.

She pours out old,
Sour, injustice;
Purging poison,
Hoarding despair.

Beloved, betrayed;
Love's vow, broken.
Ghastly sin drives
Blinders to fail.

Stabbing tears break
Tarnished diamonds.
Rose wishes she'd
Not loved at all.

Pretty Lady

There's a road out by the river,
In a dark wood where rain falls down.
There I saw him walking with her,
Pretty lady, his heart has found.

Pretty lady, you're so lovely
And I know, I was so plain but
If he's happy walking with you,
I can bury my tears today.

Pretty lady, can you hear me?
There's something that you should know.
You've got someone with that magic
To make it rain or make it snow.

Love him well and never leave him
Alone in darkness or in light,
Because he loves you. He'll not hurt you.
And if you hurt him, I'll set you right.

Pretty lady, when you hold him,
Hold him tightly, keep him from harm.
Because I love him, and he did love me,
But now it's you wrapped in his arms.

There's a road out by a river,

In a dark wood where rain falls down.

I saw him there, walking beside her,

While alone I lay my spirit down.

Spell of Parting

I hoped the world a safer place.
I feared people might be unkind.
I never asked for a safe space.
I just didn't want more lies.

You never sought reality.
You didn't ask for my advice.
You never loved my neutrality.
You never cared to be nice.

I don't begrudge your passioned speech,
Or hope you stumble into ill.
I can respect your opinions, and
I can wish you kindness still.

May all your days shine warm and bright,
And all your nights be calm and cool.
May all your needs be quickly met,
And most of your dreams come true.

May you find within yourself
A calm that allows you to be strong.
May you never see a day
When you've lived a day too long.

But as you've become who you now are,

I and you cannot abide.

And so, in all sincerity,

Please leave it rest, let time divide.

My Once Love

Thinking of you, my once love,
Of your hands, the music they played.

Your arms holding me close as
Breathlessly, you whispered my name.

You, my savior, my lover,
And I, your obedient friend.

I'll not forget what you taught
Me about me, back, before the end:

The power of letting go,
The strength in admitting to "yes,"

The relief in deciding
"No," and not trying to impress.

In time, I learned to clearly hear
The song you found in my heart.

Circumspect and ever calm,
You set me on my journey's start.

You bound me to my lost soul,
Though forever was not meant to be.

Today, my once love, I know,

You will be in each sigh I breathe.

Gems

Emerald eyes in silent rain,
Aching to be there again.
Seeing grace and being light,
Dancing to their love tonight.

Emerald eyes shine with the sting,
Black pearls breaking from the string,
Tears of hate from diamond eyes,
Cracking quartz with impure lies.

Emerald portals all closing soft,
Pyrite's dust sets soul aloft,
To heaven or down into hell,
Turquoise freezes in the well.

The Urn

Keeping the urn was a mistake.
Tossing the ashes was smart.
The golden creed would brake
The mantle brick apart.

There on the ancient wood,
Where open air should live,
The weight of ages' blood
Shifts with the urge to forgive.

Too late to say the words,
Too present to rest in peace,
The bond we worked to forge,
Too soon has been released.

We cannot fill the space,
Now that our time is done.
We already lost the race,
Are already half of one.

If I had left you here,
Without direction or desire,
What would I have you do
Once I was set afire?

I'd ask that you live on;

That you'd forgive us both our sins.

That you toss the empty urn,

Let the space fill itself in.

In time, we both will rise

Or fall if that may be.

While either heart survives,

Let life, for living be.

Fitting

They cowered in their dishwater head,
As angry words impaled their gut.
They could not survive the constant dread,
But neither could they give him up.

They'd try instead to suffer through
His impulsive, unjust rage,
While quietly wondering how long
They could both fit in their cage.

They gave up joy after he left.
Without his voice, the song did cease.
They mourned the boy. They had regrets.
But with him gone, they were released.

Before long, they recalled the truth,
Desires for adventures, unknown.
Youthful wishes for freedom and growth.
They'd custom build their fitted throne.

Rusted Heart

Tamara left just yesterday and
No one will tell me why.
If I'm laughing now it's because
I can no longer cry.

We raised all hell for years and tears and
It's completely insane
That she will never make it passed
The end of yesterday.

One old, rusted heart.
One lifetime of dreams.
One full candle burned.
One soul left to grieve.

I heard her laughter first only
Forty-seven years ago.
After the wedding of our friends
We snuck off for time alone.

She was not overtly other,
But we knew we were the same.
And, as our friendship grew,
We were roommates only in name.

Easier than we thought it would be,

We lived without a doubt.
She taught music and history
While I nursed the devout.

She was my friend for Christmas carols,
And I was her aid on trips.
We always found a way to live
Without whispers on gossips' lips.

One old, rusted heart.
One lifetime of dreams.
One full candle burned.
One soul left to grieve.

When we decided to come out
To family and close friends,
They encouraged us to be married,
Though strangers said it was a sin.

Our home got even happier
Once we didn't have to hide.
But I never spent a day with her
That wasn't filled with pride.

When Tamara left in the night,
I saw her in my dream.
Holding the homemade wedding cake

That she once shared with me.

She sat beneath an iron lamp,
Haloed in the glow.
But as it rained, rusted iron
Dripped on frosting there below.

One old, rusted heart.
One lifetime of dreams.
One full candle burned.
One soul left to grieve.

The rusted tear travelled down the side,
And off onto the grass.
But no trace of age was left on the
Sweetness as it passed.

Tamara took a bite and smiled,
Then leaned up to the lamp.
She watched the candle flicker out
Before away she danced.

She was reminding me to smile,
To not let grief stain what love had blessed.
And so, for her, I'll carry on
Until, together, we can rest.

One old, rusted heart.

One lifetime of dreams.

One full candle burned.

One soul left to grieve.

About The Author

Lucidity Lamb

Lucidity Lamb was born and raised in New England, shoveling snow and cheering for the Red Sox. Half a life later, she lives in sunny Florida with her husband. She is intentionally positive to counteract her natural tendency toward depression and anxiety. Poetry,  music, and storytelling have always been Luci's most comfortable ways of communicating her true self.

In an effort to "succeed" in the world, Luci earned a degree in Biology and an MBA, but success has a funny way of redefining itself along the way. While her career is primarily driven by structure and regulation, she pours her creativity, melancholy, morbid humor, and hope into her art. Visit her website at LucidityLamb.com.

Books By This Author

Lucid Lines; Poetry Of Truth

"Poetry of Truth" is the first chapbook of Lucidity Lamb's Lucid Lines poetry series. Luci's writing combines her innate anxiety, depression, and hope with her skills as a story-teller, resulting in a roller-coaster of relatable honesty.

Made in United States
Orlando, FL
26 May 2025

61579024R00025